ABOUT THE AUTHOR

Killian H. Gore was born in Fort Phantom in Texas in 1976. He is a distant relative of the serial killer Ellen Mort who was born in Liverpool, England and later vanished in Salt Lake City, Utah, after violently butchering all five of her husbands (*for the full true story of Ellen Mort, read my Incredible Horror Movie Facts book*).

He is the author of the short story collection Before Halloween as well as the novellas Beyond Bigfoot, The Thingy From Another World and The Demon of Heritage. His first screenplay, Blood Stained Windows, is currently viewable on Amazon Studios.

He lives in Warrington, England.

www.facebook.com/killianhgore
www.twitter.com/killianhgore

Also by Killian H. Gore

Before Halloween
The Thingy From Another World
Beyond Bigfoot
The Demon of Heritage
The Unauthorized Friday the 13th Quiz Book
The 'Burbs Unauthorized Quiz Book
Incredible Horror Movie Facts

Screenplays:

Blood Stained Windows

The Evil Dead

Unauthorized Quiz Book

By
Killian H. Gore

Contents

The Evil Dead Questions

1. At the beginning of the movie what name is written on the front of the Ford truck that almost hits the group's car?

A) Crazy Mary
B) Hairy Mary
C) Lazy Mary
D) Scary Mary

2. Which of the following is the correct description of Sam Raimi's car that features in *The Evil Dead*?

A) 1971 Delta 88 Oldsmobile
B) 1972 Delta 88 Oldsmobile
C) 1973 Delta 88 Oldsmobile
D) 1974 Delta 88 Oldsmobile

3. What is the load limit of the dangerous bridge that the group crosses in the Oldsmobile car?

A) 2 tons
B) 3 tons
C) 4 tons
D) 5 tons

4. Who composed the music score for *The Evil Dead*?

A) Danny Elfman
B) Harry Manfredini
C) Christopher Young
D) Joseph LoDuca

5. What is Ash's toast at the dinner table that Scotty translates as, "Party down"?

A) Nis, Nis, Tutarim
B) Ne, Ne, Tootle, Rim
C) Dis, Dis, Necta, Rim
D) Klaatu, Verata, Nikto

6. What is Bruce Campbell's character's full name?

A) Ashley James Williams
B) Ashley John Williams
C) Ashley Jake Williams
D) Ashley Joseph Williams

7. What was the name of the short film that Sam Raimi, Bruce Campbell and Robert Tapert made before *The Evil Dead* to help convince investors to fund the film?

A) The Book of the Dead
B) Deep in the Woods
C) Within in the Woods
D) The Cabin in the Woods

8. Which torn-up horror movie poster is visible on the wall in the cabin cellar?

A) The Texas Chain Saw Massacre
B) The Hills Have Eyes
C) Jaws
D) The Exorcist

9. Which state in America was the cabin location filmed in?

A) Michigan
B) Tennessee
C) North Carolina

D) California

10. Stephen King wrote a review of *The Evil Dead* for the November 1982 issue of Twilight Zone Magazine in which he wrote which of the following statements...?

A) The most ferociously original horror film of 1982
B) The most ferociously original horror film ever
C) The most ferociously original horror film of all time
D) The most ferociously original horror film I've ever seen

11. On the tape that the group listens to, where does the professor say they were excavating the ruins of?

A) Necronomicon
B) Sumerian
C) Demanto
D) Candar

12. Which character switches the tape recorder off when the group are listening to the tape?

A) Linda
B) Shelly
C) Ash
D) Cheryl

13. Scott (played by Richard DeManincor) went on to star in which other Sam Raimi movie as Officer Garvey?

A) A Simple Plan
B) The Gift
C) Crimewave

D) Darkman

14. After the tree-rape sequence what does Cheryl scream out when she reaches the cabin?

A) Open the door!
B) Ashley!
C) Let me in!
D) Scotty!

15. Which UK city did director Sam Raimi appear in court on obscenity charges against *The Evil Dead*?

A) Liverpool
B) London
C) Leeds
D) Leicester

16. When Linda and Shelly are playing a card-guessing game, what card is Shelly holding up that Linda incorrectly guesses as the seven of hearts?

A) Nine of diamonds
B) Two of spades
C) Jack of diamonds
D) Queen of spades

17. Which *Ash vs. Evil Dead* actress is *The Evil Dead* producer Robert Tapert married to?

A) Mimi Rogers
B) Jill Marie Jones
C) Dana DeLorenzo
D) Lucy Lawless

18. When Cheryl first becomes possessed, who does she stab in the foot with a pencil?

A) Ash
B) Scott
C) Shelly
D) Linda

19. Which famous filmmaker acted as an assistant film editor on *The Evil Dead*?

A) Joel Coen
B) Ethan Coen
C) Andy Wachowski
D) Charles Band

20. What does Shelly say to Scotty after he has dragged her out of the fireplace?

"Thank you. I don't know what I would have done if I had remained on those hot coals...

A) ... burning my pretty face"
B) ... burning my pretty flesh"
C) ... burning my pretty hair"
D) ... burning my pretty soul"

21. Which *The Evil Dead* star appeared alongside Bruce Campbell in the short *Evil Dead*-themed horror film Sam Raimi directed before *The Evil Dead*?

A) Ellen Sandweiss
B) Betsy Baker
C) Theresa Tilly
D) Richard DeManincor

22. Who of the following is NOT credited as a "Fake Shemp" in the end credits?

A) Scott Spiegel
B) Ted Raimi
C) Ivan Raimi
D) Sam Raimi

23. What does Scotty say to Ash when suggesting an alternative way to leave the cabin?

"Well, maybe there's...

A) ... an old hiking trail, or a service road, or some other way around the cliff"
B) ... another bridge, or an old road, or some other way around the cliff"
C) ... a hiking trail, or an old road, or some other way around the cliff"
D) ... an old road, or a bigger bridge, or some other way around the cliff"

24. Under what name is actress Theresa Tilly credited as in the end credits?

A) Cheryl Guttridge
B) Barbara Carey
C) Sarah York
D) Joanne Kruse

25. Who is credited as the special make-up effects artist for *The Evil Dead*?

A) Tom Savini
B) Greg Nicotero
C) Robert Kurtzman

D) Tom Sullivan

26. When the possessed Linda is sat in the doorway, how many times does Ash hit her around the head?

A) 2
B) 3
C) 4
D) 5

27. The term "Fake Shemp" is a reference to which famous comic film actors?

A) Laurel and Hardy
B) The Three Stooges
C) The Marx Brothers
D) Abbott and Costello

28. Which is the correct tagline for *The Evil Dead*?

A) The Ultimate Experience In Grueling Terror
B) Who Will Survive And What Will Be Left Of Them?
C) Death Is Just The Beginning
D) When There's No More Room In Hell, The Dead Will Walk The Earth

29. Which of the following is the correct ending to Linda's scary little song that she sings to Ash?

"We're gonna get you, we're gonna get you...

A) ... time to go to sleep, not another peep"
B) ... never gonna sleep, not another peep"
C) ... never gonna peep, never gonna sleep
D) ... not another peep, time to go to sleep"

30. Which of the *Friday the 13th* movies featured the Necronomicon (Book of the Dead) from *The Evil Dead*?

A) Freddy vs. Jason
B) Jason X
C) Jason Goes to Hell: The Final Friday
D) Jason Lives: Friday the 13th Part VI

31. Which character wears a Michigan State sweater?

A) Ash
B) Cheryl
C) Linda
D) Shelly

32. What color flowers are on the glass of water that Ash brings for Scotty before he dies?

A) Yellow
B) Red
C) Blue
D) Green

33. What is featured on the necklace box that Ash gives to Linda?

A) Two red roses
B) Two hearts
C) A unicorn
D) A crucifix

34. Who provided the voice of the professor on the tape recorder that the group listens to in the cabin?

A) John Larroquette
B) John Peakes
C) Walt Gorney
D) Bob Dorian

35. What type of chainsaw was used in the film?

A) Poulan 361
B) Stihl 066
C) Husqvarna 359
D) Homelite XL-12

36. Who play the two fishermen seen at the beginning of the film as the group travel to the cabin?

A) Ted Raimi and Sam Raimi
B) Sam Raimi and Robert Tapert
C) Scott Spiegel and Sam Raimi
D) Robert Tapert and Scott Spiegel

37. In what year was *The Evil Dead* finally released fully uncut in the UK?

A) 2000
B) 2001
C) 2002
D) 2003

38. After Linda emerges from the grave, what does she say to Ash before he chops her head off?

A) Don't kill me
B) Don't hurt me
C) We'll swallow your soul
D) I love you, Ash

39. Where was *Evil Dead: The Musical* first performed on stage?

A) New York
B) Las Vegas
C) Chicago
D) Toronto

40. When Ash is getting more ammo in the cellar he steps into a bloody puddle – what item is seen floating in that puddle?

A) Linda's necklace
B) A dead rat
C) A container of Band-Aids
D) A broken light bulb

41. Which of the following is a correct alternative title for *The Evil Dead*?

A) Headcheese
B) Twitch of the Death Nerve
C) These Bitches Are Witches
D) Dance of the Demons

42. Whose garage was used as a filming location for one of the rooms in the cellar?

A) Stephen King
B) Sam Raimi
C) Tom Sullivan
D) Ellen Sandweiss

43. What does Ash use to drag the Book of the Dead over to him before throwing it into the fire?

A) Linda's necklace
B) A severed hand
C) A chain from the cellar door
D) A tree branch

44. At which film festival did Stephen King say he first saw *The Evil Dead*?

A) Sundance Film Festival
B) Cannes Film Festival
C) Toronto Film Festival
D) Berlin Film Festival

45. Who suggested changing the name of the film to *The Evil Dead*?

A) George A. Romero
B) Tom Savini
C) Bruce Campbell
D) Irvin Shapiro

46. In which year did *The Evil Dead* begin principal photography?

A) 1981
B) 1980
C) 1978
D) 1979

47. What did the crew call the camera effect in which the camera would slide on a mount covered with gaffer tape and smeared with lubricant?

A) Vas-o-Cam
B) Ram-o-Cam
C) Sam-o-Cam

D) Shaky-Cam

48. A grand premiere for *The Evil Dead* (complete with a gimmicky ambulance outside the venue) was held at which theater in Detroit?

A) Colonial Theater
B) State Theater
C) Redford Theater
D) Senator Theater

49. When the cast and crew finished filming at the cabin, they buried something in the hole they'd dug out for the cellar – what was it?

A) The Book of the Dead prop
B) A severed head prop
C) A time capsule
D) Linda's necklace

50. What does the final POV (shaky-cam) shot of the film begin on?

A) The sky
B) A grave with a wooden cross
C) A tree stump
D) A leaf

Who was Bruce Campbell's, Sam Raimi's and Ellen Sandweiss' high school drama teacher at Groves High School in Michigan?

A) Simon Nuchtern
B) Jim Moll
C) Sheila Roberts
D) Carol Valenti

The Evil Dead Answers

1) C - Lazy Mary
2) C - 1973 Delta 88 Oldsmobile
3) B - 3 tons
4) D - Joseph LoDuca
5) A - Nis, Nis, Tutarim
6) A - Ashley James Williams
7) C - Within in the Woods
8) B - The Hills Have Eyes
9) B – Tennessee
10) A - The most ferociously original horror film of 1982
11) D - Candar
12) D – Cheryl
13) C - Crimewave
14) B - Ashley!
15) C - Leeds
16) A - Nine of diamonds
17) D - Lucy Lawless
18) D - Linda
19) A - Joel Coen
20) B – "... burning my pretty flesh"
21) A - Ellen Sandweiss
22) D - Sam Raimi
23) C – "... a hiking trail, or an old road, or some other way around the cliff"
24) C - Sarah York
25) D - Tom Sullivan
26) B – 3
27) B - The Three Stooges
28) A - The Ultimate Experience In Grueling Terror
29) D – "... not another peep, time to go to sleep"
30) C - Jason Goes to Hell: The Final Friday
31) C - Linda
32) A - Yellow
33) B - Two hearts
34) D - Bob Dorian
35) D - Homelite XL-12

36) B - Sam Raimi and Robert Tapert
37) B - 2001
38) A - Don't kill me
39) D – Toronto
40) C - A container of Band-Aids
41) C - These Bitches Are Witches
42) B - Sam Raimi
43) A - Linda's necklace
44) B - Cannes Film Festival
45) D - Irvin Shapiro
46) D - 1979
47) A - Vas-o-Cam
48) C - Redford Theater
49) C - A time capsule (according to Bruce Campbell the time capsule is in a cigar box wrapped in tape containing a burned out light bulb, a piece of the fake wooden beam used to beat Linda over the head with, a piece of gaffer tape and a code by Sam Raimi to unlock the "visual meaning" of *The Evil Dead*)
50) D - A leaf

Deadite Hard Bonus Question!

B - Jim Moll

Evil Dead II
Questions

1. What is the name of the phony distribution company at the beginning of the movie?

A) Orchid Releasing Corporation
B) Poppy Releasing Corporation
C) Redwood Releasing Corporation
D) Rosebud Releasing Corporation

2. In the opening narration, what year did the Necronomicon Ex-Mortis (*roughly translated, The Book of the Dead*) disappear?

A) 1100 AD
B) 1200 AD
C) 1300 AD
D) 1400 AD

3. What does Ash tell Linda they will say to the owners of the cabin if they should come back?

A) They got lost
B) They're friends of the family
C) Their car broke down
D) They ran out of gas

4. Who went on from *Evil Dead II* to work on the QVC home shopping TV channel?

A) Richard Domeier
B) Sarah Berry
C) Denise Bixler
D) Kassie Wesley DePaiva

5. Why did the filmmakers reshoot the opening recap scenes of the film?

A) The original negatives had been destroyed in a fire

B) They wanted to shoot on 35mm film instead of 16mm
C) They wanted to change certain story elements
D) They didn't have the rights to the footage from *The Evil Dead*

6. In the flashback scene of Professor Raymond Knowby translating the Book of the Dead, what is Henrietta doing in the background on the rocking chair?

A) Reading
B) Knitting
C) Drinking
D) Eating

7. Where was the interior of the cabin set built?

A) On Bruce Campbell's ranch
B) In an abandoned mall
C) In a school gym
D) In an aircraft hangar

8. Which four people recorded the commentary track for *Evil Dead II*?

A) Sam Raimi, Bruce Campbell, Ivan Raimi and Howard Berger
B) Sam Raimi, Ted Raimi, Bruce Campbell and Robert Tapert
C) Sam Raimi, Bruce Campbell, Scott Spiegel and Greg Nicotero
D) Bruce Campbell, Scott Spiegel, Greg Nicotero and Robert Tapert

9. Which production member played the airport worker who struggled to open the door of the airplane that Annie and Ed disembark?

A) Robert Tapert
B) Sam Raimi
C) Greg Nicotero
D) Scott Spiegel

10. The exterior cabin location was built in the same location that was used for which other movie?

A) Always
B) The Color Purple
C) Empire of the Sun
D) Twilight Zone: The Movie

11. After Linda rises from the grave, what does she say to Ash when she appears in front of him at the cabin?

A) Play with me
B) Dance with me
C) Kiss me
D) Hello, lover

12. Which Hollywood star asked Bruce Campbell to say, "Work shed" to him when they were shooting a movie together?

A) Tim Robbins
B) Jim Carrey
C) Tobey Maguire
D) Kurt Russell

13. Which actress is said to have inspired the character of Bobby Joe?

A) Frances McDormand
B) Molly Ringwald
C) Daphne Zuniga
D) Holly Hunter

14. A prop from a famous horror movie appears on a number of occasions throughout *Evil Dead II*, notably when Ash cuts up Linda in the work shed, but what is this prop?

A) Sentinel Sphere
B) Lemarchand's puzzle box
C) Freddy Krueger's glove
D) Jason Voorhees' hockey mask

15. Actress Sarah Berry (Annie) went on to star in which other horror film sequel?

A) Fright Night Part 2
B) C.H.U.D. II – Bud the Chud
C) Return of the Living Dead II
D) Bride of Re-Animator

16. Before financing *Evil Dead II*, Dino De Laurentiis was interested in having Sam Raimi direct which Stephen King adaptation?

A) Pet Sematary
B) It
C) Thinner
D) The Tommyknockers

17. What amount of money does Jake primarily ask for (before Bobby Joe nudges him) to take Annie and Ed on the trail to the cabin?

A) 45 dollars
B) 50 dollars
C) 20 dollars
D) 35 dollars

18. What is the name of the special effects make-up company that three of the make-up artists from *Evil Dead II* went on to form?

A) Magical Media Industries
B) Creature Effects, Inc.
C) Reel Efx, Inc.
D) KNB EFX Group

19. When Ash's possessed hand is smashing plates over his head in the kitchen, what packet of food falls onto the floor?

A) Saltines
B) Triscuits
C) Pop Tarts
D) Lucky Charms

20. Which of the following is an authentic tagline from *Evil Dead II*?

A) Just when you thought it was safe to be dead
B) Kiss Your Nerves Good-bye!
C) The Ultimate Horror Experience!
D) So you think you're lucky to be alive...

21. What was the name of the movie Sam Raimi directed before *Evil Dead II*?

A) Blood Simple
B) Crimewave
C) Intruder
D) The Dead Next Door

22. As Jake, Ed, Bobby Joe and Annie walk along the trail to the cabin, which character does NOT have a flashlight?

A) Ed
B) Bobby Joe
C) Jake
D) Annie

23. Director of Photography Peter Deming went on to shoot which other *Evil Dead*-themed horror movie?

A) Cabin Fever
B) My Name is Bruce
C) Tucker and Dale vs. Evil
D) The Cabin in the Woods

24. What book is on the top of the pile of books that Ash places on top of the can containing his severed hand?

A) The Hand of Ethelberta
B) A Farewell to Arms
C) Cheiro's Language of the Hand
D) Arms and the Man

25. Which of the following storylines was dropped from the final version of the script?

A) Escaped convicts hiding in the cabin, burying their loot in the cellar and being torn to pieces by Henrietta

B) Escaped convicts burying their loot next to the cabin and returning to dig up Linda's severed head instead

C) Escaped convicts finding the cabin and attempting to steal The Book of The Dead to sell to a wealthy collector

D) Escaped convicts asking Ash to help them hide from the Sheriff who is on their trail

26. After Ash has fired the shotgun at the wall to shoot his possessed hand, what does he say?

A) Gotcha, didn't I? You little sucker!
B) Gotcha, didn't I? You stupid sucker!
C) Gotcha, didn't I? You lousy sucker!
D) Gotcha, didn't I? You silly sucker!

27. Which three *Evil Dead II* actors had roles in Sam Raimi's *Oz the Great and Powerful*?

A) Sarah Berry, Kassie Wesley DePaiva and Denise Bixler
B) Richard Domeier, John Peakes and Lou Hancock
C) Bruce Campbell, Ted Raimi and Dan Hicks
D) Bruce Campbell, Richard Domeier and Ted Raimi

28. Which writer's work is the Book of the Dead (Necronomicon) inspired by?

A) Bram Stoker
B) Edgar Allan Poe
C) H.P. Lovecraft
D) Richard Matheson

29. When various objects are hysterically laughing in the cabin, Ash joins in and mimics the movements of which one of them?

A) The deer head
B) The cellar door
C) The curtains
D) The gooseneck lamp

30. Who shares a screenwriting credit with Sam Raimi for *Evil Dead II*?

A) Ivan Raimi
B) Scott Spiegel
C) Robert Tapert
D) Bruce Campbell

31. Which item in the cabin makes Annie believe Ash has killed her parents?

A) A chainsaw
B) A shotgun
C) A severed hand
D) The Book of the Dead

32. Who played the possessed Henrietta?

A) Ivan Raimi
B) Ted Raimi
C) Lou Hancock
D) Josh Becker

33. When Henrietta recounts to Annie about her date of birth, what date does she give?

A) September 2nd, 1962
B) September 3rd, 1962
C) September 4th, 1962
D) September 5th, 1962

34. Who wrote a draft of the script that was entirely discarded?

A) Stephen King
B) Tom Holland
C) Mick Garris
D) Josh Becker

35. What was the name of the short horror film that inspired the possessed hand sequence in *Evil Dead II*?

A) The Incredible Helping Hand
B) The Evil Hand
C) Attack of the Helping Hand
D) Night of the Living Hand

36. Which attribute helped actress Sarah Berry to be cast in the role of Annie Knowby?

A) Her background in archeology
B) Her knowledge of demonology
C) Her previous horror film roles
D) Her scream

37. Which character gets Henrietta's eyeball in their mouth?

A) Annie
B) Bobby Joe
C) Jake
D) Ash

38. What lullaby does Henrietta sing to Annie?

A) Brahm's Lullaby
B) Twinkle, Twinkle, Little Star

C) Hush, Little Baby
D) All Through The Night

39. What does Ash say to Annie before going down into the fruit cellar to retrieve the necessary pages from the Book of the Dead?

"Then lets head down into that cellar...

A) ... and kill ourselves a witch"
B) ... and carve ourselves a witch"
C) ... and slice ourselves a witch"
D) ... and slay ourselves a witch"

40. Whose skeletal remains fall on Ash in the fruit cellar when he is retrieving the missing pages from the Book of the Dead?

A) Professor Raymond Knowby
B) Linda
C) Bobby Joe
D) Jake

41. Where was *Evil Dead II* predominately filmed?

A) Mt. Airy, North Carolina
B) Blairstown, New Jersey
C) North Tonawanda, New York
D) Wadesboro, North Carolina

42. Who was the special make-up effects supervisor on the film?

A) Mark Shostrom
B) Screaming Mad George
C) Rick Baker

D) Tom Savini

43. Who worked on the stop-motion special effects for *Evil Dead II*?

A) Ray Harryhausen
B) Tom Sullivan
C) Phil Tippet
D) Peter Kleinow

44. Score composer Joseph LoDuca went on to score which Sam Raimi produced horror film?

A) The Grudge
B) Boogeyman
C) Poltergeist
D) 30 Days of Night

45. What does Annie say the second passage from the Book of the Dead will do?

A) Open a vortex and suck the evil away
B) Open a gateway and send the evil back
C) Open a rift and send the evil back
D) Open an entrance and send the evil back

46. When Ash chainsaws the Rotten Apple Head demon in the eye, what color liquid oozes from it?

A) Red
B) Green
C) Yellow
D) Blue

47. What is Annie's dying word?

A) Nos-feratos
B) Amen-non
C) Kanda
D) Ak-adeem

48. When Ash arrives in the medieval setting, what does one of the knights exclaim?

A) Slay the beast! 'Tis a demon!
B) Slay the beast! 'Tis a deadite!
C) Slay the beast! 'Tis a devil!
D) Slay the beast! 'Tis a demonite!

49. Who portrays the knight who delivers the line, "Hail he who has come from the skies to deliver us from the terrors of the deadites"?

A) Don Campbell
B) Richard Grove
C) Timothy Patrick Quill
D) Sam Raimi

50. What is the 2000 documentary directed by Robert A. Ferretti on the making of *Evil Dead II* called?

A) Groovy Gore
B) The Gore the Merrier
C) A Little Bit Gore
D) Dead by Dawn

What is the name of the script supervisor whose name was mistakenly omitted from the end credits of *Evil Dead II*?

A) Andra Barbuica
B) Ludivine Doazan
C) Francoise Charlap
D) Sophie Boyer

Evil Dead II
Answers

1) D - Rosebud Releasing Corporation
2) C - 1300 AD
3) C - The car broke down
4) A - Richard Domeier
5) D - They didn't have the rights to the footage from *The Evil Dead*
6) B - Knitting
7) C – In a school gym (the J.R. Faison Junior High School in Wadesboro, North Carolina)
8) C - Sam Raimi, Bruce Campbell, Scott Spiegel and Greg Nicotero
9) A - Robert Tapert
10) B - The Color Purple
11) B - Dance with me
12) D - Kurt Russell (whilst filming *Escape from L.A.*)
13) D - Holly Hunter (she was also considered for the role of Bobby Joe)
14) C - Freddy Krueger's glove
15) B - C.H.U.D. II – Bud the Chud
16) C - Thinner
17) A - 45 dollars
18) D - KNB EFX Group
19) A - Saltines
20) B - Kiss Your Nerves Good-bye!
21) B - Crimewave
22) C - Jake
23) D - The Cabin in the Woods
24) B - A Farewell to Arms
25) B - Escaped convicts burying their loot next to the cabin and returning to dig up Linda's severed head instead
26) A - Gotcha, didn't I? You little sucker!
27) C - Bruce Campbell, Ted Raimi and Dan Hicks
28) C - H.P. Lovecraft
29) D – The gooseneck lamp
30) B - Scott Spiegel
31) A - A chainsaw

32) B - Ted Raimi
33) A - September 2nd, 1962
34) D - Josh Becker
35) C - Attack of the Helping Hand
36) D - Her scream
37) B - Bobby Joe
38) C - Hush, Little Baby
39) B - "… and carve ourselves a witch"
40) D - Jake
41) D - Wadesboro, North Carolina
42) A - Mark Shostrom
43) B - Tom Sullivan
44) B - Boogeyman
45) C - Open a rift and send the evil back
46) D - Blue
47) C - Kanda
48) B - Slay the beast! 'Tis a deadite!
49) D - Sam Raimi
50) B - The Gore the Merrier

Deadite Hard Bonus Question!

C - Francoise Charlap

Army of Darkness Questions

1. In the flashback scene to Ash in the S-Mart department store, what section is he seen working in?

A) Housewares
B) Firearms
C) DIY
D) Pharmacy

2. Which Hollywood star portrays Linda in *Army of Darkness*?

A) Holly Hunter
B) Jennifer Jason Leigh
C) Michelle Pfeiffer
D) Bridget Fonda

3. Which horror movie star appeared in *Army of Darkness* as the Deadite Captain?

A) Kane Hodder
B) Robert Englund
C) Bill Moseley
D) Jeffrey Combs

4. How does Duke Henry the Red introduce himself to Ash?

A) Duke of Shale, Lord of the Northlands and leader of its peoples
B) Duke of the Shire, Lord of the Eastlands and leader of its peoples
C) Duke of York, Lord of the Westlands and leader of its peoples
D) Duke of Sherwood, Lord of the Southlands and leader of its peoples

5. Whose name was misspelled on one of the theatrical posters for *Army of Darkness*?

A) Robert Tapert (as *Robert Tappert*)
B) Embeth Davidtz (as *Embeth Daviditz*)
C) Bruce Campbell (as *Bruce Cambell*)
D) Joe LoDuca (as *Joe DoLuca*)

6. After the old lady says, "Into the pit with those bloodthirsty sons of whores," what food does she bite into?

A) An apple
B) A loaf of bread
C) A meat drumstick
D) A bunch of grapes

7. How many deadites does Ash fight whilst in the pit he has been thrown into?

A) 1
B) 2
C) 3
D) 4

8. How does Ash describe his "boomstick" to the crowd outside the castle?

A) 12 gauge double-barreled Beretta
B) 12 gauge double-barreled Merkel
C) 12 gauge double-barreled Remington
D) 12 gauge double-barreled Zabala

9. In which US state was *Army of Darkness* filmed in?

A) New Mexico

B) Texas
C) Arizona
D) California

10. During the fight with the possessed witch, which character grabs an axe off the wall in the castle?

A) Blacksmith
B) Wiseman
C) Shelia
D) Ash

11. Ian Abercrombie (Wiseman) went on to star in which *Jurassic Park* movie?

A) Jurassic Park
B) The Lost World: Jurassic Park
C) Jurassic Park III
D) Jurassic World

12. What object does Ash crush with his newly constructed mechanical hand?

A) Wine bottle
B) Knight's helmet
C) Metal goblet
D) Skull

13. A studio battle over the rights to which other horror franchise delayed the release of *Army of Darkness*?

A) Halloween
B) Hannibal Lecter
C) Amityville
D) Frankenstein

14. When Shelia gives Ash a gift that she has made for him, what does Ash refer to it as?

A) A toilet cleaner
B) A napkin
C) A handkerchief
D) A horse blanket

15. Certain storyboards from which other film were used to orchestrate the battle scenes in *Army of Darkness*?

A) Zulu (1964)
B) Lawrence of Arabia (1962)
C) Spartacus (1960)
D) Joan of Arc (1948)

16. The words that Ash is instructed to recite to obtain the Book of the Dead (*Klaatu verata nikto*) are a variation of a phrase from which classic science fiction film?

A) Invaders from Mars
B) Forbidden Planet
C) The Day the Earth Stood Still
D) The Thing From Another World

17. The credited co-editor R.O.C Sandstorm is actually a pseudonym for who?

A) Robert Tapert
B) Scott Spiegel
C) Ivan Raimi
D) Sam Raimi

18. In the windmill scene, what do the evil Mini-Ash group poke Ash in the butt with?

A) A fork
B) A knife
C) A spoon
D) A screwdriver

19. Which zombie movie is actress Patricia Tallman (Possessed Witch) also known for?

A) Return of the Living Dead
B) Night of the Living Dead
C) House of the Dead
D) Land of the Dead

20. What nursery rhyme does Ash sing in the windmill to the Mini-Ashes?

A) Itsy Bitsy Spider
B) London Bridge Is Falling Down
C) Humpty Dumpty
D) The Grand Old Duke of York

21. How many Books of the Dead does Ash have to choose from in the cemetery?

A) 1
B) 2
C) 3
D) 4

22. In the Director's Cut version of *Army of Darkness*, the cave in which Ash drinks the magic potion was famously used in which superhero television show?

A) Adventures of Superman
B) The Flash
C) Batman

D) Superboy

23. When Ash is trying to recall the final word he's supposed to say to obtain the Book of the Dead, what does he say?

A) Necktie, nectar, nickel, noodle
B) Nightie, nighthawk, ninja, nipple
C) Netball, nougat, neon, needle
D) Nutmeg, nicker, number, nibble

24. Why did a new ending for the film have to be shot?

A) The negatives were damaged in post-production
B) The filmmakers wanted to set-up story elements to a sequel
C) The test audiences didn't like it
D) The studio didn't like the original downbeat ending

25. When Ash is resurrected as Evil Ash, what does he say?

A) Groovy
B) Hail to the King, baby
C) I got a bone to pick with you
D) I live again

26. Which actor's father was killed on-screen in *Army of Darkness*?

A) Bill Moseley's
B) Ted Raimi's
C) Bruce Campbell's
D) Richard Grove's

27. When Ash returns to the castle with the Book of the Dead, who is grabbed and flown away by a winged deadite?

A) Shelia
B) Ash
C) Wiseman
D) Blacksmith

28. What was the estimated budget for *Army of Darkness*?

A) $12 million
B) $13 million
C) $14 million
D) $15 million

29. What does Evil Ash say to Shelia when the deadites bring her over to him?

A) Groovy
B) Give me some sugar, baby
C) This is my boomstick
D) Well hello, Mr. Fancypants

30. Why does Sam Raimi say they reshot Ash cutting his hand of with a chainsaw in the opening recap sequence?

A) The original was too gory
B) They didn't have the rights to the footage
C) They couldn't locate the original negatives
D) The original scene was the wrong pace

31. What is *Army of Darkness* actually titled as in the opening credits?

A) Bruce Campbell vs. The Medieval Dead
B) Ash vs. Evil Dead
C) Bruce Campbell vs. Army of Darkness
D) Ash vs. Army of Darkness

32. When a knight tells Lord Arthur that an army of the dead are gathered in the wilderness and are approaching the castle, how many days ride does he say they are away?

A) 1
B) 2
C) 3
D) 4

33. The animated skeletons in *Army of Darkness* are an homage to a scene from which Ray Harryhausen movie?

A) Clash of the Titans
B) Sinbad and the Eye of the Tiger
C) Jason and the Argonauts
D) The Golden Voyage of Sinbad

34. Which actor delivers the line, "You can count on my steel"?

A) Sam Raimi
B) Ted Raimi
C) Timothy Patrick Quill
D) Richard Grove

35. Who composed the "March of the Dead" theme music for *Army of Darkness*?

A) Danny Elfman
B) Ennio Morricone

C) Elmer Bernstein
D) Howard Shore

36. Who says the line, "I may be bad, but I feel good"?

A) Evil Ash
B) Shelia
C) Deadite Captain
D) Ash

37. What is the name of the special effects process involving a variation on front-projection that was used on *Army of Darkness*?

A) Introversion
B) Back/Front Projection
C) Introvision
D) Beamvision

38. What brand of soda is visible in the trunk of Ash's car?

A) Coca Cola
B) Pepsi
C) Tab
D) Mountain Dew

39. When the army of the dead arrives at the castle what does Ash say?

"Maybe, just maybe my boys can stop them from getting that book...

A) ...yeah, maybe I'm a loud-mouthed braggart"
B) ... yeah, maybe I'm a Chinese jet pilot"
C) ... yeah, maybe I'm out of my depth"

D) ... yeah, maybe I'm a store clerk"

40. Who is *Army of Darkness* dedicated to in the end credits?

A) Laurence Olivier
B) Anthony Quayle
C) John Cassavetes
D) Irvin Shapiro

41. What is the first fired from the castle at the army of the dead?

A) Catapults of blazing fireballs
B) Jets of fire from Ash's modified car
C) Explosive arrows
D) Gunshots from Ash's shotgun

42. Actress Embeth Davidtz (Shelia) went on star in which Steven Spielberg movie?

A) Saving Private Ryan
B) Jurassic Park
C) A.I. Artificial Intelligence
D) Schindler's List

43. What is the phrase that Evil Ash struggles to say on account of his jaw constantly falling out of place?

A) Sally forth
B) Tally ho
C) March on
D) Go get 'em

44. Who provided the voice of the deadite who says, "Let's get the hell out of here!"?

A) Sam Raimi
B) Scott Spiegel
C) Bruce Campbell
D) Ted Raimi

45. What weapon does the possessed Shelia attack Ash with during the battle at the castle?

A) A chainsaw
B) A spear
C) A sword
D) An axe

46. How is Evil Ash finally killed?

A) Pushed from the castle into a fire
B) Fired into the air with an exploding catapult
C) Cut to pieces by the propeller on Ash's car
D) Ash sets him on fire with a torch

47. In the US Theatrical version of the movie, what must Ash do in order to return to his own time?

A) Read aloud a passage from the Book of the Dead
B) Destroy the Book of the Dead
C) Drink a potion and say, "Klaatu verata nikto"
D) Swallow six drops of a potion

48. In the US Theatrical version of the movie, what does the deadite pick up to use as a weapon in the S-Mart store at the end of the film?

A) A cash register
B) A microwave oven

C) A toaster
D) A mini fridge

49. In the US Theatrical version of the movie, what is the final line of dialogue spoken by Ash?

A) Give me some sugar, baby
B) Just me, baby. Just me
C) Hail to the King, baby
D) Groovy

50. What happens to Ash in the original ending to *Army of Darkness* featured in the Director's Cut and UK Theatrical Cut version of the movie?

A) He wakes up back at the cabin and hears Linda in the other room playing the tape recording of Professor Knowby translating the Book of the Dead
B) He wakes up in a padded cell and it is revealed that he is a patient in a lunatic asylum
C) The potion doesn't work and he is stuck in 1300 AD forever
D) He sleeps for too long and awakes in a post-apocalyptic landscape

Deadite Hard Bonus Question!

In Bill Warren's *The Evil Dead Companion* book, what is the chapter on the making of *Army of Darkness* called?

A) Ancient Blood
B) The Medieval Dead
C) Evil Dead 3
D) The Ultimate Experience in Medieval Horror

Army of Darkness Answers

1) A - Housewares
2) D - Bridget Fonda
3) C - Bill Moseley
4) A - Duke of Shale, Lord of the Northlands and leader of its peoples
5) D - Joe LoDuca (as *Joe DoLuca*)
6) B - A loaf of bread
7) B - 2
8) C - 12 gauge double-barreled Remington
9) D - California
10) A – Blacksmith
11) B - The Lost World: Jurassic Park
12) C - Metal goblet
13) B - Hannibal Lecter
14) D - A horse blanket
15) D - Joan of Arc (1948)
16) C - The Day the Earth Stood Still
17) D - Sam Raimi
18) A - A fork
19) B - Night of the Living Dead
20) B - London Bridge Is Falling Down
21) C - 3
22) C - Batman
23) A - Necktie, nectar, nickel, noodle
24) D - The studio didn't like the original downbeat ending
25) D - I live again
26) C - Bruce Campbell's (Charlie Campbell)
27) A - Shelia
28) B - $13 million
29) B - Give me some sugar, baby
30) D - It was the wrong pace
31) C - Bruce Campbell vs. Army of Darkness
32) B - 2
33) C - Jason and the Argonauts
34) B - Ted Raimi
35) A - Danny Elfman

36) B - Shelia
37) C - Introvision
38) A - Coca Cola
39) B – "... yeah, maybe I'm a Chinese jet pilot"
40) D - Irvin Shapiro
41) C - Explosive arrows
42) D - Schindler's List
43) A - Sally forth
44) D - Ted Raimi
45) B - A spear
46) B - Fired into the air with an exploding catapult
47) C - Drink a potion and say, "Klaatu verata nikto"
48) A - A cash register
49) C - Hail to the King, baby
50) D - He sleeps for too long and awakes in a post-apocalyptic landscape

Deadite Hard Bonus Question!

A - Ancient Blood

Evil Dead
Questions

1. At the beginning of the film, what does the girl say to her father when it first becomes apparent that she is demonically possessed?

A) I will rip your soul out, daddy
B) I will rip your soul apart, daddy
C) I will tear your soul apart, daddy
D) I will swallow your soul, daddy

2. Which country was *Evil Dead* filmed in?

A) Australia
B) Canada
C) New Zealand
D) USA

3. What does David say the necklace he gives to Mia is made from?

A) Hawthorn tree
B) Buckthorn tree
C) Willow tree
D) Elder tree

4. Who is NOT one of the film's producers?

A) Bruce Campbell
B) Scott Spiegel
C) Sam Raimi
D) Robert Tapert

5. What does David cite as a reason he didn't visit his and Mia's dying mother?

A) He had just got job at a garage in Detriot
B) He had just got job at a garage in Flint
C) He had just got job at a garage in Knoxville

D) He had just got job at a garage in Chicago

6. What is the Book of the Dead referred to as by the characters in *Evil Dead*?

A) Necronomicon
B) Naturom Demonto
C) Necronomicon Ex-Mortis
D) Book of the Dead

7. When Eric and David first go down into the cellar, what does Eric say the room smells like?

A) Burnt hair
B) Rotting meat
C) Dead animals
D) Burnt butt hair

8. Who from the original *Evil Dead* films was initially reluctant for the film to be remade?

A) Sam Raimi
B) Robert Tapert
C) Bruce Campbell
D) Tom Sullivan

9. When Eric reads the incantation from the Book of the Dead what is the first word he utters?

A) Kunda
B) Astratta
C) Montosse
D) Canda

(*Please note that reading these words aloud may result in demonic possession!*)

---

10. What was the tagline for *Evil Dead* on the original theatrical poster?

A) How do you kill what's already dead?
B) The most terrifying film you will ever experience
C) They know what scares you
D) What you know about fear... doesn't even come close

11. What is the name of David and Mia's dog?

A) Ash
B) Grandad
C) Grandpa
D) Granny

12. What country is director Fede Alvarez originally from?

A) Brazil
B) Argentina
C) Paraguay
D) Uruguay

13. What is inscribed in the Book of the Dead that explains Mia's strange behavior in the shower?

A) Boiling water on the flesh
B) Burn the witch
C) Burn the demon
D) Boiling water on the body

14. When David drives Mia away from the cabin, what prevents them from leaving the woods?

A) The bridge had been destroyed
B) The car breaks down
C) The creek has flooded
D) David swerves to avoid a demon and ends up in a pond

15. In which monster-themed movie did actor Lou Taylor Pucci (Eric) go on to star in?

A) Winter
B) Spring
C) Summer
D) Autumn

16. Which character shuts the cellar door on Mia after she has vomited blood onto Olivia's face?

A) Eric
B) Olivia
C) David
D) Natalie

17. *Evil Dead* voice artist Rupert Degas (Demon Voice) also provided demonic voices for which other horror film?

A) The Exorcism of Emily Rose
B) The Last Exorcism
C) Exorcist: The Beginning
D) The Devil Inside

18. Eric doesn't believe Mia is having a panic attack – what is he scared her behavior is connected to?

A) The Book of the Dead
B) The evil spirits in the woods

C) The witchcraft in the basement
D) The voodoo in the basement

19. What does the possessed Olivia repeatedly stab Eric in the face with?

A) A shard of glass
B) A nail
C) A knitting needle
D) A hypodermic needle

20. Which two actors from the original *The Evil Dead* are listed in the end credits as "Voices from the original Evil Dead".

A) Bruce Campbell and Bob Dorian
B) Ellen Sandweiss and Bob Dorian
C) Betsy Baker and Bob Dorian
D) Richard DeManincor and Bob Dorian

21. What does the possessed Mia use to slice her own tongue in half with?

A) A scalpel
B) A razor blade
C) An electric knife
D) A utility knife

22. What is the end of the passage from the Book of the Dead that Eric reads out to David?

"Once he feasts on five souls, the sky will bleed again and the abomination...

A) ... will rise from Hell"
B) ... will rise from the grave"
C) ... will bring Hell on Earth"

D) ... will walk the Earth"

23. Before being hired to direct *Evil Dead*, what was the name of Fede Alvarez's short film that impressed the film's producers?

A) Monster
B) Alive in Joburg
C) Panic Attack!
D) Factory Farmed

24. Which character's hand becomes demonically possessed in *Evil Dead*?

A) Olivia's
B) David's
C) Eric's
D) Natalie's

25. As written in the Book of the Dead, which of the following is NOT listed as a way to cleanse and purify the possessed?

A) A live burial
B) Decapitation
C) Bodily dismemberment
D) Purification by fire

26. What is the name of the television comedy series that actress Jane Levy (Mia) starred in as Tessa Altman?

A) New Girl
B) Suburgatory
C) 2 Broke Girls
D) Awkward.

27. In order to instill a true sense of fear in actor Shiloh Fernandez (David) what did the director tell him to do?

A) Go and watch *The Exorcist* alone in his trailer
B) Go and write down a list of things that truly scared him
C) Go and sit for 15 minutes in an actual abandoned cabin near the set
D) Go off into the woods alone at night for 15 minutes

28. How many nails does the possessed Natalie shoot into David's leg?

A) 2
B) 3
C) 4
D) 5

29. An extended cut of the film infamously aired in the UK on which TV channel?

A) BBC 2
B) Horror Channel
C) Channel 4
D) Channel 5

30. After David has shot Natalie's other arm off, what does she say to him?

A) David, why are you hurting me?
B) Please David, don't hurt me
C) David, you're hurting my pretty flesh
D) I love you, David. Why are you hurting me?

31. What do the letters of the main character's names spell out?

A) DEVIL
B) SATAN
C) DEMON
D) BEAST

32. What is the lullaby that Mia sings to David before he's about to set the cabin alight?

A) Baby, Sweet Baby
B) Baby, Little Baby
C) Hush, Little Baby
D) Hush, Sweet Baby

33. In which country was *Evil Dead* banned due to the high level of violence, blood and gore?

A) United Kingdom
B) Norway
C) Ireland
D) Ukraine

34. What does Eric hit the possessed Mia over the head with to save David from drowning in the cellar?

A) A spade
B) An axe
C) A crowbar
D) A hammer

35. What line from the original *The Evil Dead* appeared in the 2013 *Evil Dead* trailer but was cut from the finished film?

A) For God's sake, what happened to her eyes?
B) You bastards, why are you torturing me like this?

C) We're gonna get you, not another peep, time to go to sleep
D) Come unlock this chain and let me out. I'm all right now

36. What color dress does David put onto Mia before he buries her?

A) Red
B) Floral
C) Green
D) Blue

37. What original prop from *The Evil Dead* was given to the filmmakers by Robert Tapert for use in the remake?

A) The deer head
B) The wall clock
C) Linda's necklace
D) The cellar door

38. After the possessed Mia has told David that their mother hates him, what does she say next?

A) "She sucks cocks in Hell"
B) "She wants you to join us in Hell"
C) "She waits for you down here"
D) "She waits for you in Hell"

39. Director Fede Alvarez went on to direct an episode of which horror TV show in 2014?

A) The Walking Dead
B) From Dusk Till Dawn
C) American Horror Story
D) The Strain

40. When David goes back into the cabin to get the car keys, what does he pause to look at?

A) The Book of the Dead
B) Natalie's severed arm
C) A photograph on the wall
D) The necklace he gave to Mia

41. Which comedy film directly spoofed scenes from *Evil Dead*?

A) The Hungover Games
B) A Haunted House
C) A Haunted House 2
D) Scary Movie 5

42. What does David say to Mia before he shuts himself in the cabin before setting it on fire?

A) Get the hell out of here
B) Go, save yourself
C) Leave me
D) Get out of here

43. How does David start the fire in the cabin?

A) He lights a match on spilt gasoline
B) He throws his lighter onto spilt gasoline
C) He shoots a canister of gasoline with the shotgun
D) He shoots a gas pipe over the oven with the shotgun

44. What is unusual about the performer who is credited as playing the Abomination Mia?

A) She's played by a man
B) She's played by an amputee

C) She's played by an actress considered for the role of Mia
D) She's entirely computer generated

45. When Bruce Campbell appears as Ash after the end credits have rolled, what does he say?

A) Hail to the king, baby
B) Groovy
C) Give me some sugar, baby
D) Felt like someone just walked over my grave

46. In the work shed, what weapon does Mia almost choose before opting for the chainsaw?

A) A shotgun
B) A machete
C) A hammer
D) A nail gun

47. What does Abomination Mia say to Mia when her hand is trapped under the car during the climatic scene?

A) You're gonna die here, you little bitch
B) You're gonna die here, and join us in Hell
C) You're gonna die here, and burn in Hell
D) You're gonna die here, you pathetic junkie

48. How many gallons of fake blood were said to have been used for the "raining blood" scene at the end of the movie?

A) 40,000
B) 50,000
C) 60,000
D) 70,000

49. What does the final shot of the film, before the end credits, finish on?

A) The Book of the Dead opening
B) A demonic hand shooting out from the ground
C) The Book of the Dead closing shut
D) A POV shot racing through the woods into Mia's face

50. What alternative ending for *Evil Dead* was filmed but not used in the final cut of the film?

A) POV crashing through the cabin and slamming into Mia
B) A possessed, badly burned David emerging from the cabin
C) Mia being dragged by demon hands into the ground
D) Mia walking along a road and being picked up by a man in a truck

<u>Deadite Hard Bonus Question!</u>

Who did an uncredited script revision on the *Evil Dead* screenplay?

A) Diablo Cody
B) Joss Whedon
C) Quentin Tarantino
D) Carrie Fisher

Evil Dead
Answers

1) A - I will rip your soul out, daddy
2) C - New Zealand
3) B - Buckthorn tree
4) B - Scott Spiegel
5) D - He had just got job at a garage in Chicago
6) B - Naturom Demonto
7) A - Burnt hair
8) C - Bruce Campbell
9) A - Kunda
10) B - The most terrifying film you will ever experience
11) C - Grandpa
12) D - Uruguay
13) D - Boiling water on the body
14) C - The creek has flooded
15) B - Spring
16) A – Eric
17) C - Exorcist: The Beginning
18) C - The witchcraft in the basement
19) D - A hypodermic needle
20) B - Ellen Sandweiss and Bob Dorian
21) D - A utility knife
22) A – "… will rise from Hell"
23) C - Panic Attack!
24) D - Natalie's
25) B – Decapitation
26) B - Suburgatory
27) D - Go off into the woods alone at night for 15 minutes
28) B - 3
29) C - Channel 4
30) A - David, why are you hurting me?
31) C - DEMON
32) B - Baby, Little Baby
33) D - Ukraine
34) C - A crowbar

35) C - We're gonna get you, not another peep, time to go to sleep
36) A - Red
37) B - The wall clock
38) D - "She waits for you in Hell"
39) B - From Dusk Till Dawn
40) C - A photograph on the wall
41) D - Scary Movie 5
42) D - Get out of here
43) C - He shoots a canister of gasoline with the shotgun
44) A - She's played by a man (Randal Wilson)
45) B - Groovy
46) B - A machete
47) D - You're gonna die here, you pathetic junkie
48) B - 50,000
49) C - The Book of the Dead closing shut
50) D - Mia walking along a road and being picked up by a man in a truck

Deadite Hard Bonus Question!

A - Diablo Cody

My Name is Bruce Questions

1. What Bruce Campbell-themed T-shirt is Jeff (Taylor Sharpe) wearing at the beginning of the movie?

A) Bubba Ho-Tep
B) The Evil Dead
C) Man with the Screaming Brain
D) Maniac Cop

2. What is the name of the Oregon mining town in which the film is set?

A) Gold Dust
B) Gold Lick
C) Gold Valley
D) Gold Creek

3. On the set of *Cavealien 2*, what drink does Bruce Campbell ask the crewmember Tiny for?

A) Lemonade
B) Bitter Lemon
C) Lemon and limewater
D) Lemon water

4. How many characters does Ted Raimi play in *My Name is Bruce*?

A) 2
B) 3
C) 4
D) 5

5. When Campbell is having a drink with his agent in the strip bar, which horror film character does he make a reference to?

A) Freddy Krueger
B) Pinhead
C) Candyman
D) Leprechaun

6. What is the name of the fictional brand of whiskey that Bruce drinks in his trailer?

A) Sam's
B) Shemp's
C) Stooges
D) Sugar's

7. What is the name of the documentary by Michael Kallio on the making of *My Name is Bruce*?

A) 30 Days in Hell
B) Fear of Guan-Di
C) The Shocking Untruth
D) Heart of Dorkness

8. Which actress from the original *Evil Dead* films played Bruce Campbell's ex-wife Cheryl?

A) Ellen Sandweiss
B) Denise Bixler
C) Betsy Baker
D) Sarah Berry

9. In the town hall meeting, which of Bruce Campbell's films does Bruce mention in reference to disasters?

A) Alien Apocalypse
B) Icebreaker
C) Terminal Invasion

D) Assault on Dome 4

10. According to Jeff, what does the bottle of "Evil Dead Shampoo" that Bruce uses in the shower actually contain?

A) Bleach
B) Hot sauce
C) A urine sample
D) Drain cleaner

11. What drink does Bruce ask Kelly for at the bar?

A) A Southern Screw
B) A Sex on the Beach
C) A Slow Screw against the Wall
D) A Screaming Orgasm

12. What is the name of the movie that Bruce tells Kelly he made whilst still in high school?

A) Within the Woods
B) Blade of the Skull Ripper
C) Shemp Eats the Moon
D) It's Murder!

13. Where were the exteriors of the town filmed?

A) On Bruce Campbell's property in Oregon
B) In the town of Jacksonville, Oregon
C) In a ghost town in Oregon
D) On a sound stage in Oregon

14. Why does Bruce opt not to use the chainsaw that Jeff has had specially made for him?

A) It's too dangerous
B) It's too heavy
C) It's too noisy
D) It's too cliché

15. What animal does Bruce throw out of the car that he has stolen from an old lady?

A) A dog
B) A cat
C) A parrot
D) A goldfish

16. Which *My Name is Bruce* performer appeared in Sam Raimi's early film, *It's Murder!*?

A) Dan Hicks
B) Ellen Sandweiss
C) Ben McCain
D) Timothy Patrick Quill

17. When Ted the Sign Painter is killed by Guan-Di, what number does he add to the population sign?

A) 0
B) 1
C) 2
D) 3

18. What was the proposed name for the *My Name is Bruce* sequel that Bruce Campbell expressed interest in making?

A) Bruce vs. Ash
B) Bruce vs. Dracula
C) Bruce vs. Satan

D) Bruce vs. Frankenstein

19. What is the name of Bruce Campbell's dog in the movie?

A) Ash
B) Sam n' Rob
C) Henrietta
D) Sammy

20. What are the two scripts that Bruce receives in the post when he returns to his trailer?

A) Evil Dead 4 and 5
B) Cavealien 3 and 4
C) Moontrap 2 and 3
D) Mindwarp 3 and 4

21. Who drives Bruce Campbell from his trailer back to the mining town?

A) Kasey
B) Kelly
C) Jeff
D) Mills

22. What sport is Wing (Ted Raimi) watching on TV when Kelly enters his cabin to take his bean curd?

A) Sumo wrestling
B) Ice Hockey
C) Chess
D) Bowling

23. What does Bruce say to Kelly and Jeff before they kill Guan-Di together?

A) Give me some sugar, baby
B) Let's go slay ourselves a demon
C) Who's for Chinese?
D) I'll never forgive you for dragging me out here

24. After Bruce, Kelly and Jeff defeat Guan-Di, what is Bruce's last request to Jeff?

A) Next time, give Sam Raimi a call
B) Next time, call that Xena chick
C) Next time, call that Buffy chick
D) Next time, give Hercules a call

25. What short scene happens after the end credits?

A) A POV camera races toward Bruce
B) Guan-Di slays the McCain Brothers
C) Bruce returns to his cabin and is attacked by Guan-Di
D) Guan-Di slays the Dirt Farmer and Frank

<u>Deadite Hard Bonus Question!</u>

Who played Guan-Di in *My Name is Bruce*?

A) Ronald P. Zwang
B) James J. Peck
C) Stephen A. White
D) Jeffrey Scott Kindred

My Name is Bruce Answers

1) A - Bubba Ho-Tep
2) B - Gold Lick
3) D - Lemon water
4) B – 3 (Mills Toddner/Wing/Ted The Sign Painter)
5) C - Candyman
6) B - Shemp's
7) D - Heart of Dorkness
8) A - Ellen Sandweiss
9) D - Assault on Dome 4
10) D - Drain cleaner
11) C - A Slow Screw against the Wall
12) B - Blade of the Skull Ripper
13) A - On Bruce Campbell's property in Oregon
14) B - It's too heavy
15) B - A cat
16) D - Timothy Patrick Quill
17) A - 0 (changing the population number to 330)
18) D - Bruce vs. Frankenstein
19) B - Sam n' Rob (obviously a reference to Sam Raimi and Robert Tapert)
20) B - Cavealien 3 and 4
21) A – Kasey (the singing prostitute)
22) D - Bowling
23) D - I'll never forgive you for dragging me out here
24) C - Next time, call that Buffy chick
25) B - Guan-Di slays the McCain Brothers

Deadite Hard Bonus Question!

B - James J. Peck (Peck also played the Cavealien Monster in *My Name is Bruce* as well as designing and creating Guan-Di's mask)

Drag me to Hell Questions

1. After the boy is dragged to Hell at the beginning of the movie, what does the young Shaun San Dena say?

A) I will see you in Hell
B) This is not the end
C) We will meet again
D) I will save your soul

2. What is the rare collectable item that Christine gives to Clay in his office?

A) A stamp
B) A baseball card
C) A button
D) A coin

3. When Mrs. Ganush attacks Christine in her car, what object does Christine thrust into her mouth?

A) A ruler
B) A stapler
C) A pencil
D) A calculator

4. When Christine visits the fortuneteller, Rham Jas, what fact does he first give about her during the reading?

A) You have a cat
B) Your mother is an alcoholic
C) You're about to get a promotion
D) You work with money

5. Where does Clay say to Christine that they could visit together on the weekend?

A) His parent's farm in Santa Barbara
B) His parent's cabin in Santa Barbara
C) His parent's cabin in Tennessee
D) His parent's beach house in San Diego

6. Which actress was initially cast as Christine but had to drop out for scheduling reasons?

A) Emma Stone
B) Kirsten Dunst
C) Ellen Page
D) Maggie Gyllenhaal

7. What does Christine scream at Stu after he's asked her for some help with loan procedures?

A) Get your dirty hands off my desk
B) Get your filthy pig knuckle off my desk
C) Get your grubby paws off my desk
D) Get your piggy trotters off my desk

8. When Christine revisits Rham Kas, what does he tell her the name of the evil spirit is that plagues her?

A) Legion
B) Leyak
C) Lelin
D) Lamia

9. What role does Ted Raimi play in *Drag me to Hell*?

A) Doctor
B) Bank Guard
C) 19th Century Ghost
D) Chef

10. Who composed the music score for the film?

A) Danny Elfman
B) Joseph LoDuca
C) Christopher Young
D) Marc Streitendfeld

11. What animal does Christine end up killing as a sacrifice?

A) A chicken
B) A goat
C) A cat
D) A rabbit

12. Which Sam Raimi regular turned down a role in *Drag me to Hell* because of a scheduling conflict?

A) Tobey Maguire
B) Bruce Campbell
C) James Franco
D) J.K. Simmons

13. What type of cake does Christine bring as a gift to Clay's parents house?

A) Fruitcake
B) Chocolate cake
C) Devil's food cake
D) Harvest cake

14. What was Sam and Ivan Raimi's first title for the *Drag me to Hell* script?

A) 3 Days of Hell
B) The Button

C) The Curse
D) The Evil Curse

15. What does Christine do at the dinner table at Clay's parents house before she throws a glass at the door?

A) She spews blood into Clay's mothers face
B) She coughs up a fly
C) She has a nosebleed all over the table
D) She vomits onto her cake

16. How much money in cash does Rham Jas say Christine will need to hire the services of the medium he knows?

A) $5,000
B) $10,000
C) $15,000
D) $20,000

17. What phrase is Christine told to repeatedly chant during the séance?

A) Release the demon from my soul
B) The power of Christ compels you
C) I welcome the demon into my soul
D) I welcome the dead into my soul

18. During the ritual at the medium's house, who is tasked with slaying the goat?

A) Milos
B) Christine
C) Rham Jas
D) Shaun San Dena

19. In what role does director Sam Raimi make a cameo as?

A) Mourner at Death Feast
B) Bank Customer
C) Ghost at Séance
D) Family at Diner

20. When Christine attempts to give Stu her cursed button, who does Stu worry that she will tell about his recent deceitful behavior at the bank?

A) His mom
B) His dad
C) His wife
D) His parole officer

21. What is the name of the cemetery where Christine goes to give the button to the deceased Mrs. Ganush?

A) Oakwood Cemetery
B) Highgate Cemetery
C) Eternal Peace Cemetery
D) Resurrection Cemetery

22. Where does Christine leave the envelope containing the button (or so she thinks) on Mrs. Ganush's dead body?

A) In her pocket
B) In her mouth
C) On her forehead
D) In her hand

23. What was the name of the similarly themed horror movie that actress Alison Lohman also appeared in?

A) The Exorcism of Emily Rose
B) The Last Exorcism
C) The Vatican Tapes
D) The Devil Inside

24. Where is Christine finally "dragged to hell"?

A) On a railway station platform
B) In the cemetery
C) On a railroad track
D) In Shaun San Dena's house

25. *Drag me to Hell* features a piece of music that was originally composed (but not used) for which other horror film?

A) The Omen
B) Rosemary's Baby
C) The Devil Rides Out
D) The Exorcist

<u>Deadite Hard Bonus Question!</u>

What is the license plate on Mrs. Ganush's car?

A) 99951
B) 15666
C) 231959
D) 66613

Drag me to Hell
Answers

1) C - We will meet again
2) D - A coin
3) A - A ruler
4) D - You work with money
5) B - His parent's cabin in Santa Barbara (Clay mentions that it's surrounded by trees and is private - a reference to the *Evil Dead* cabin)
6) C - Ellen Page
7) B - Get your filthy pig knuckle off my desk
8) D - Lamia
9) A – Doctor
10) C - Christopher Young
11) C - A cat
12) B - Bruce Campbell
13) D - Harvest cake
14) C - The Curse
15) B - She coughs up a fly
16) B - $10,000
17) D - I welcome the dead into my soul
18) A - Milos
19) C - Ghost at Séance
20) B - His dad
21) A - Oakwood Cemetery
22) B - In her mouth
23) C - The Vatican Tapes
24) C - On a railroad track
25) D - The Exorcist

Deadite Hard Bonus Question!

A – 99951 (which when turned upside down reads IS666. It's also worthy of note that the car is the classic Oldsmobile from nearly every Sam Raimi movie)

Sam Raimi Questions

1. What is Sam Raimi's middle name?

A) Michael
B) Matthew
C) Marshall
D) Mason

2. Which Coen brothers film did Raimi co-write with Joel and Ethan Coen?

A) Miller's Crossing
B) Blood Simple
C) The Hudsucker Proxy
D) Raising Arizona

3. Aside from his work in Hollywood, Sam's brother Ivan also works in which other profession?

A) Lawyer
B) Dentist
C) Stockbroker
D) Doctor

4. In which of these Stephen King television mini-series did Sam Raimi appear?

A) The Shining
B) It
C) The Tommyknockers
D) Storm of the Century

5. Years before Raimi made the *Spider-Man* movies he met with Stan Lee to pitch which other superhero movie to 20th Century Fox?

A) Daredevil

B) Hulk
C) Iron Man
D) Thor

6. Which Sam Raimi film received a Best Actor in a Supporting Role Oscar nomination?

A) The Gift
B) A Simple Plan
C) For Love of the Game
D) The Quick and the Dead

7. Who did Raimi direct a music video for in 1988?

A) David Bowie
B) Alice Cooper
C) Iggy Pop
D) Billy Idol

8. In which of these John Landis movies did Sam Raimi have a cameo as a Drive-In Security Guard?

A) Spies Like Us
B) Beverly Hills Cop III
C) Coming to America
D) The Blues Brothers

9. Which horror film director appeared in *The Quick and the Dead* as one of Young Herod's men?

A) Wes Craven
B) Mick Garris
C) Tobe Hooper
D) Clive Barker

10. Which of Sam Raimi's films spawned an unaired television pilot?

A) The Quick and the Dead
B) A Simple Plan
C) The Gift
D) Darkman

11. In which Raimi film did composer Danny Elfman appear as the character Tommy Lee Ballard?

A) Spider-Man
B) The Gift
C) A Simple Plan
D) Darkman

12. Which of Raimi's films was co-written with the Coen brothers?

A) A Simple Plan
B) The Gift
C) Crimewave
D) The Quick and the Dead

13. Who is the only lead actor from *The Evil Dead* not to have a cameo appearance in Raimi's *Oz the Great and Powerful*?

A) Richard DeManincor
B) Ellen Sandweiss
C) Betsy Baker
D) Theresa Tilly

14. In what country was *Ash vs. Evil Dead* filmed in?

A) Canada
B) USA
C) UK
D) New Zealand

15. What baseball team does Kevin Costner's character play for in Raimi's *For Love of the Game*?

A) Boston Red Sox
B) New York Yankees
C) Detroit Tigers
D) Chicago Cubs

16. Which actress was in talks to star in Raimi's aborted *Spider-Man 4* as the Black Cat?

A) Scarlett Johansson
B) Anne Hathaway
C) Emma Stone
D) Zoe Saldana

17. Which television series did Raimi direct two episodes of in 2014?

A) Rake
B) The Walking Dead
C) Bates Motel
D) Hannibal

18. What is the name of the horror film production company that Sam Raimi set up with Robert Tapert?

A) Dark Castle Entertainment
B) Ghost House Pictures
C) Twisted Pictures

D) Rogue Pictures

19. In which summer-camp-based movie did Sam Raimi play the character Stick Coder?

A) Wet Hot American Summer
B) Poison Ivy
C) Heavy Weights
D) Indian Summer

20. Which of the following is the correct tagline for Raimi's *A Simple Plan*?

A) Small town. Big crime. Dead cold
B) A lot can happen in the middle of nowhere
C) Sometimes good people do evil things
D) An ordinary place, an extraordinary thriller

21. In *Spider-Man*, who is the owner of Sam Raimi's classic Oldsmobile car?

A) Peter Parker
B) Norman Osborn
C) Ben Parker
D) Mary Jane Watson

22. Who was initially sought for the lead role in *Oz the Great and Powerful* before James Franco landed the part?

A) Robert Downey Jr.
B) Tobey Maguire
C) Bruce Campbell
D) Jim Carrey

23. Who is the main villain in Raimi's *Spider-Man 2*?

A) Sandman
B) Doctor Octopus
C) Venom
D) Lizard

24. How many sequels were there to *Darkman*?

A) 1
B) 2
C) 3
D) 4

25. In an interview with MTV News, which horror film did Raimi cite as his favorite scary movie?

A) Bride of Frankenstein (1935)
B) Psycho (1960)
C) The Exorcist (1973)
D) The Haunting (1963)

Deadite Hard Bonus Question!

What was Sam Raimi's original German family surname?

A) Regenbogen
B) Reingewertz
C) Riese
D) Reuter

Sam Raimi
Answers

1) C - Marshall
2) C - The Hudsucker Proxy
3) D - Doctor
4) A - The Shining
5) D - Thor
6) B - A Simple Plan (for Billy Bob Thornton)
7) C - Iggy Pop (Raimi directed the *Cold Metal* music video)
8) A - Spies Like Us
9) B - Mick Garris
10) D - Darkman
11) B - The Gift
12) C - Crimewave
13) A - Richard DeManincor
14) D - New Zealand
15) C - Detroit Tigers
16) B - Anne Hathaway
17) A - Rake
18) B - Ghost House Pictures
19) D - Indian Summer
20) C - Sometimes good people do evil things
21) C - Ben Parker
22) A - Robert Downey Jr.
23) B - Doctor Octopus
24) B – 2 (*The Return of Durant* and *Die, Darkman, Die*)
25) D - The Haunting (1963)

Deadite Hard Bonus Question!

B - Reingewertz

Bruce Campbell Questions

1. What was the name of the first feature film that Bruce Campbell directed?

A) Man with the Screaming Brain
B) My Name is Bruce
C) Alien Apocalypse
D) Lunatics: A Love Story

2. Which John Carpenter film did Bruce Campbell star in?

A) Ghosts of Mars
B) Vampires
C) Escape From L.A.
D) Memoirs of an Invisible Man

3. What is Bruce Campbell's autobiography called?

A) Make Love! The Bruce Campbell Way
B) Shame and Perversion: The Bruce Campbell Story
C) If Chins Could Kill: Confessions of a B Movie Actor
D) My Chin Can Hurt People

4. In which TV series did Bruce Campbell star in as the character Sam Axe?

A) Jack of All Trades
B) Burn Notice
C) The Replacements
D) Hercules: The Legendary Journeys

5. In which Michael Crichton film adaptation did Campbell appear in?

A) Sphere
B) Timeline

C) Congo
D) The 13th Warrior

6. What was the name of the character Campbell played in Sam Raimi's *Oz the Great and Powerful*?

A) Winkie Gate Keeper
B) Elder Tinker
C) Mayor of The Emerald City
D) Quadling Scarecrow Maker

7. In which computer-animated film did Bruce Campbell provide the voice for the character of Fugax?

A) Cars 2
B) Antz
C) Cloudy with a Chance of Meatballs
D) The Ant Bully

8. In which television sitcom did Bruce have a recurring role?

A) Roseanne
B) Ellen
C) Grace Under Fire
D) Will & Grace

9. What was the name of the Western television series that Campbell starred in from 1993 to 1994?

A) Harts of the West
B) Deadwood
C) The Adventures of Brisco County, Jr.
D) Hawkeye: The First Frontier

10. What is the title of the proposed _Bubba Ho-Tep_ sequel that Campbell has said he won't star in?

A) Bubba Ho-Tep 2
B) Bubba Dracula: Curse of the She-Vampires
C) Elvis vs. Frankenstein
D) Bubba Nosferatu: Curse of the She-Vampires

11. In which Coen brothers movie did Bruce Campbell star in as the character Smitty?

A) The Big Lebowski
B) The Man Who Wasn't There
C) O Brother, Where Art Thou?
D) The Hudsucker Proxy

12. Bruce Campbell was originally intended to play Vic Ajax in _Crimewave_ but, as a result of studio interference, which role did he end up playing?

A) Renaldo "The Heel"
B) Faron Crush
C) Arthur Coddish
D) Ernest Trend

13. Which Deep Purple track is used in the first season trailer for _Ash vs. Evil Dead_?

A) Burn
B) Space Truckin'
C) Smoke on the Water
D) Highway Star

14. Who directed Campbell in the film _Maniac Cop_?

A) William Lustig
B) Larry Cohen
C) Sam Raimi
D) Josh Becker

15. In *Bubba Ho-Tep* Bruce Campbell plays Elvis Presely, but who does his co-star Ossie Davis portray?

A) Abraham Lincoln
B) Martin Luther King, Jr.
C) Malcolm X
D) JFK

16. What was Bruce Campbell's character in *Xena: Warrior Princess* and *Hercules: The Legendary Journeys* called?

A) Joxer
B) Borias
C) Autolycus
D) Ares, God of War

17. Which of the following is NOT one of the credited roles Campbell portrayed in Sam Raimi's *Spider-Man* trilogy?

A) Tour Guide
B) Ring Announcer
C) Snooty Usher
D) Maître d'

18. In which *From Dusk Till Dawn* did Campbell appear?

A) From Dusk Till Dawn
B) From Dusk Till Dawn 2: Texas Blood Money

C) From Dusk Till Dawn 3: The Hangman's Daughter
D) From Dusk Till Dawn: The Series

19. Which country did Campbell film *Man with the Screaming Brain* in?

A) Romania
B) Luxembourg
C) Czech Republic
D) Bulgaria

20. In which of Sam Raimi's movies were Bruce Campbell's scenes completely cut from the theatrical release of the film?

A) The Gift
B) A Simple Plan
C) The Quick and the Dead
D) For the Love of the Game

21. For which film did Bruce Campbell record the DVD commentary "in character"?

A) Army of Darkness
B) Man with the Screaming Brain
C) Bubba Ho-Tep
D) Evil Dead II

22. Which of Bruce Campbell's films features Jake "The Raging Bull" LaMotta in an acting role?

A) Terminal Invasion
B) Icebreaker
C) Sundown: The Vampire in Retreat
D) Maniac Cop

23. What was the name of the tornado movie in which Campbell played a storm chaser?

A) Tornado!
B) Tornado Alley
C) Metal Tornado
D) Tornado Warning

24. In which Lucky McKee horror film did Bruce Campbell have a starring role?

A) The Woman
B) The Woods
C) May
D) All Cheerleaders Die

25. Sam Raimi and Bruce Campbell were both born in which city in Michigan?

A) Battle Creek
B) Royal Oak
C) Traverse City
D) East Lansing

As Bruce Campbell is an ordained minister he is licensed to marry people, but who does he say was the strangest couple he ever married?

A) A couple dressed as Ash and Linda from *The Evil Dead*
B) A couple dressed as zombies
C) A couple dressed as vampires
D) A couple dressed as aliens

Bruce Campbell
Answers

1) A - Man with the Screaming Brain
2) C - Escape From L.A.
3) C - If Chins Could Kill: Confessions of a B Movie Actor
4) B - Burn Notice
5) C - Congo
6) A - Winkie Gate Keeper
7) D - The Ant Bully
8) B - Ellen
9) C - The Adventures of Brisco County, Jr.
10) D - Bubba Nosferatu: Curse of the She-Vampires
11) D - The Hudsucker Proxy
12) A - Renaldo "The Heel"
13) B - Space Truckin'
14) A - William Lustig
15) D - JFK
16) C - Autolycus
17) A - Tour Guide
18) B - From Dusk Till Dawn 2: Texas Blood Money
19) D - Bulgaria
20) C - The Quick and the Dead
21) C - Bubba Ho-Tep (Campbell recorded the commentary track "in character" as Elvis Presley)
22) D - Maniac Cop
23) A - Tornado!
24) B - The Woods
25) B - Royal Oak

Deadite Hard Bonus Question!

B – A couple dressed as zombies (Bruce officiated the "zombie wedding" marriage of Nathan Patrick Dooley and Casey Russell in a ceremony at ZomBcon in Seattle in 2010)

Acknowledgements

I would like to offer my thanks to all of the Evil Dead websites I have browsed during the writing of this quiz book as well as IMDb, Wikipedia, Facebook, *The Evil Dead Companion* by Bill Warren, *If Chins Could Kill: Confessions of a B Movie Actor* by Bruce Campbell and the Blu-ray releases of *The Evil Dead, Evil Dead II, Army of Darkness, Evil Dead, My Name is Bruce* and *Drag me to Hell*.

Special thanks to the Book of the Dead creator himself, Mr. Tom Sullivan, and the author of The Evil Dead Companion, Mr. Bill Warren, for answering questions for my upcoming book, *What's Your Favorite Scary Movie?*

To my fellow Evil Dead fans, I hope you've had a groovy time answering the questions in this book. I've worked hard to make sure that all of the information is absolutely correct. But if you do find anything that you don't agree with then you know where to find me. Hiding under my desk.

Best wishes, Killian

www.ingramcontent.com/pod-product-compliance
Lightning Source LLC
Chambersburg PA
CBHW060404290526
45791CB00002B/601